Pieces
of
Stone

For Teresa. "The Real Teresa" .whom I've come to know and appreciate.

John Vincent Stone

Pieces of Stone

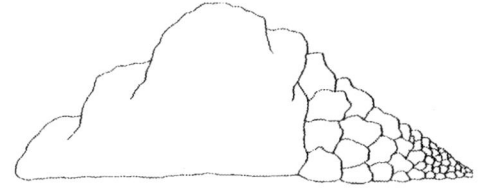

JOHN VINCENT STONE

Copyright © 2003 by John Vincent Stone.

Library of Congress Number: 2003095142

ISBN: Hardcover 1-4134-2262-4
Softcover 1-4134-2261-6

All rights reserved. No part of this book may be reproduced or transmitted in any form or by any means, electronic or mechanical, including photocopying, recording, or by any information storage and retrieval system, without permission in writing from the copyright owner.

This book was printed in the United States of America.

To order additional copies of this book, contact:
Xlibris Corporation
1-888-795-4274
www.Xlibris.com
Orders@Xlibris.com
20229

CONTENTS

Introduction 15

CHAPTER 1
Enter Herein

Enter Herein 19
Pieces of Me 21
Beneath The Rafters 22
Welcome 23
Inside View 24
God's Apology 25
Mothers 26
Fathers 27
Sons 28
Daughters 29
Destiny's Captain 30
The Note 31
No Such Thing 32
All in Awe 33
Compassion 35
Eventual friends 36
But a Moment 38
The Seed 39

CHAPTER 2
Us

Us 43
Friendship 44

Who Are You? 45
An Air About You 46
In My Dreams? 47
A Trace of Innocence 48
Beasts 49
Missed Demeanor 50
Silence Speaks 51
Swallowing your pride 53
Toons 54
Same ol' song and dance 55
When You're Gone 56
Warriors 57
Of 58
Beached 60
Bovine 61

CHAPTER 3
I know You

I Know You 65
Toilet 67
For Laughing 68
Monsters 69
Give and Take 70
Ugly Face 71
Once Uttered 72
A Passing Thought 73
The Mark of Cain 74
Zombie 75
The Memory People 76
Looking Back 77
Splitting Image 78
Where were you when midnight came? 79
The Edge 80
Footfalls 82

CHAPTER 4
Evolution

Evolution	87
Is It You?	88
Love	91
What Love is . . .	92
Passion's Fire	94
Secret Valentine	96
Conquestion	97
Extremes	98
Dark Eyes	100
Wishes	102
Protection	103
While The World Aged One more Night	104
Just Like You	106
When Onions Bloom	107
Night Storm	108
'Cause	109

CHAPTER 5
Through The Bars

Through The Bars	113
Schtik	114
I	115
A Letter to Me	116
Twins	118
Note Withstanding	119
Peripheral Division	120
Credo	121
The Navigator	122
The best you can do . . .	123
Pity pot	124
All We Are	125

Teacher 126
Seers 127
The Climb 128
The Question 129
Determinations 130

CHAPTER 6
Thousand Islands

Thousand Islands 135
A Time of Blue 139
Stone's Extremity 141
Shadowland 142
Simplicity 145
Complications 147
Enigma 148
Gods 150
The Fax 151
Criticism 153
A Hard Act to Follow 154
The Task 155
Coagulation 156

CHAPTER 7
The Thin Line

The Thin line 161
Tolerance vs Toleration 162
Power 164
Trying 165
The Standard 167
Endurance 169
Bite your tongue! 170
Busybody 173
Oblique 174
To be clear 176

Doubt	178
The pursuit of excellence . . .	179
The greater burden . . .	180
Convict	182
Zeal	183
Timidity	184
The Sophists	185
Generations	186
Conceptions	187

CHAPTER 8
What's in a Name?

What's in a name?	191
Joe & Rose	192
Romeo & Juliet	194
The Doll House	195
The Butterfly	196
Raisins of Regret	197
Life and Death	198
Convictions . . .	201
Flames	202
Ashes	204
The Grate society	207
Alzheimer	208
Loss	209
Desperation	210
Blood Vain	211
Defense of Reason	212
Cabins	213

CHAPTER 9
Losin' It

Losin' it	219
The Race for the Throne	221

Somersault	223
Beam Me Up!	224
Reality Revisited	226
Think About It!	227
Pour it on!	228
Shuns	229
Only Sometimes	230
Well, Yes and No	231
Just In Case	232
Jest In Case	234
Hindsight	235
In The Cool, Gray, Dawn	236
Odd, Man	237
Jester's Misfortune	238

CHAPTER 10
Nothins

Nothins	243
The Wise Man's Fool	244
Anger	245
The Touch	246
Pandora's Box	247
More or Less	248
Regret	249
The Mighty Might	250
Determinator	251
Little Pewter Dragon	252
Above All Else	253
Whispers	254

Index	257

Dedication

This book is dedicated to Judi for her steadfast belief in me
and in these pieces of myself, to Marla
for her much needed critical encouragement in the beginning,
and to my children from whom I have learned so much,
and from whom I have inherited at least some of my insanity.

I would like to acknowledge the efforts of Mr. Joseph L. Hunt, the artist, for his rendition of my Pieces of Stone logo. I think that the public will see his work in the near future and learn to appreciate it, as I do.

Introduction

In this book you'll find essays, poetry, not necessarily poetry, and social commentary. There may be some pieces you like and others you don't. But I think you'll find that most of them provoke thought. Thought, by itself, does not produce results. Provocation does.

As far as the mechanics of this work are concerned, I believe in the premise that, in writing, there are no rules.

Since rules that do not exist cannot be broken, I offer . . .
Pieces of Stone.

John Vincent Stone

Chapter 1
Enter Herein

Enter Herein

Come . . . if you've lived life.
Enter . . . there is much to recognize.
For there is much of life contained herein.

Even if you haven't been to the dark side,
haven't lived down where the river runs deep
and the cold wind blows . . .
come. You may see ahead of your time,
more, much more than you know.

Enter herein, this quiet world,
where the unspoken word is master.
Come, learn the power of silence.

Experience with me,
a little joy, a little sorrow,
and a small view of possible tomorrows.
This stuff we call life.
From each fleeting thought we leave behind
to the woeful burden so heavy on the mind.
From that philosophical rush we sometimes feel
to the push of reality at the edge where we kneel.

Ignore the grasping hands and blank staring face
of a clock that never sleeps.
It has no power here.

Let the by-gone bury its dead,
for now is all that matters.
Now is always the season to learn.
This it is, and always was.
Herein, begin,
just between us.

Pieces of Me

Pieces of Stone.
Pieces of me.
Chipped one by one from among
what I've thought, who I've known, what I've seen.

Many edges, so sharp and rough,
smoothed by wind, fire, and rain just enough
to allow me to enjoy feeling the heat of the Sun,
see the twinkle of the stars for what they are,
look reflectively into the night, and know
that life is, indeed, good,
but only if we make it so.

With the sweat of ink having dried so recklessly
on these pages, I hope that you will find,
despite all our differences
and in spite of the turmoil that indifference often causes,
and all the things that each of us have separately known,
that we are, even so, much the same.
You. Me. And these Pieces of Stone.

Beneath The Rafters

Though our days are numbered,
falling from the calendar, one by one,
always reminding us of our limitations;
we must look beyond the obvious
to find the subtle, deep rooted contentment
softly proclaimed in the quiet times
by those for whom we care.

Tears of sorrow stain the memory.
Those of joy cleanse the soul.
As warm hands tug at the heartstrings,
grasping for protection from the cold.

Even when the rafters rattle with intimidation
from the world that surrounds us
and the floor quakes because of the discontentment
we feel because of it . . .

We need to fill our hearts with truth
in a life so short
that can only be learned from the value
of those closest to us
and fill our arms with the swell of compassion
that can be found
only when we embrace them.

Welcome

If your passage through these doors is peaceful,
peace be with you.

If your attitude is at least tolerable, welcome.

If your hands are honest and your heart is good,
make yourself at home.

But

If you've come to disrupt and cause division
among our ranks.

If you're here to steal our sleep like a hunger in the dark,
causing pain in refrains of evil from the heart.

All I can say, is go away.

Inside View

Realize, I'm alive.
Started back then, don't know when.
Hear sounds, turn around.
Feel hand, can't stand.
Kick my feet, other's treat.
Shortly after, hearing laughter.
Kick again, never know when.
Know no other, but my mother.
Pretty soon, out of room.
Want to shout, "let me out!"
Stretching feet, grit no teeth.

Feeling strange, things change.
Feeling stronger, home gets longer.
Being routed, feeling crowded.
Moving on, water gone.
Walls close in, make me thin.
Courage lack, want to go back!
Too late, sealed fate.
Can't stay, on my way.
Weathered storm. I am born.

God's Apology

Children...
are God's apology
to those
who had to grow up.

A tug
on heartstrings
grown old.

A joy
to those
who deserve them.

And a curse
to the ones
who don't.

Mothers

Most mothers have an ability, unseen and unheard,
by those in her charge.
Which (though invisible and silent) makes for
a responsibility so large . . .
that the big things which make the little ones
seem so small . . .
become little things, after all.

She's able to put importance in its place.
Finding what strength is, in a presumed weakness
which helps those around her reach for their capacity
by stretching a hope that she has tied around them
to greater lengths than they might have otherwise known.
Making a mother, possibly, the tightest
and most secure bond they'll ever know.

While they'll probably never realize
what it was that made them feel so.

Fathers

Hear me lift my voice in anger!
See me clench my fists above me!
Feel my tension in the air
to protect those I love
who love me.
Hear me roar my warnings out
in the face of intimidation.
Beating back the world's attack
for my family's preservation.

Then . . .
see me calm myself
in the ashes of life's retreat,
to hold a hand and dry a tear,
which, makes my life complete.

There is no need to fear me,
I'm but a humble man, and still,
though I do not live with anger raised,
it's enough to know I can . . . and will!

Sons

When they're little,
it's why this, and why that?
Why? Why? Why?

But . . . as they grow older,
sons are the ones who take the dares.
Share a pact with consequence.
Wearing chance like circumstance, gone awry.
So hardly seeing reason.
So seldom asking . . . why?

Till the season of procreation
swells from within.
Makes them hesitate, confused by daily transfusions.
Tinglings of new feelings, never felt before.
When, they discover girls.

Then, my friend . . . it begins all over again.

Daughters

They are the glitter that hides
in an uncut diamond.

They start out with giggles,
and mature to jiggles
that draw the most disgusting creatures on Earth
to a door
where a father frowns, a mother sighs,
and a girl turns her head and rolls her eyes,
more proud of her choice than ever.

Where, in the balance,
hangs the fringe of life anew.
Which begins
with less than complete approval
for choices made by . . . a daughter.

Destiny's Captain

We are the masters of our own destinies,
much as the captain of a great sailing ship.
But, are subject to the elements
and must determine when to drop our sails
and brave the storm.

As when the captain was a child,
looking out to sea,
we must realize that our children
dream of the day
when they, too, can sail away.

It's our responsibility to teach them
what we've learned from experience,
so that when they set out on their own adventures,
they also can brave the storm.

The Note

The note said, "be noteworthy, be strong.
Be able to withstand anything that could go wrong."
It said, "be understanding, while standing firm, honest,
and always willing to keep your word."

The note said, "I know you can't always be here,
but please, always come home,
without the antagonism I've heard about from other kids,
and the mumbles of undertone."

It said, "I'm telling you this, because I know I can,
from all the times I've felt your hand on mine,
squeezing just enough
to expose a determined look in your eye.
A silent strength that will teach me that things
don't always work out the way we think they should,
still, that you've always done your best for me
and always will.
Which will encourage my own best efforts."

It said all this and more.
The note.
That note.
A shapeless scrap of tablet paper
with only three words scrawled in crayon blue,
that said, simply, "I Luv You."

No Such Thing

When dealing with little kids
there is no such thing as a stupid question.

Sometimes a child will ask a question
simply because he or she *does* want to know the answer.
But, so very often a question may be an attempt
to be a part of a world they know so little about.
Possibly, because they just want to be close.

Those adults who have never thought of it in this way
can open channels they didn't know existed, simply
by paying attention.

Those who ignore their children, are indeed poor,
because they have no answers to give.

All in Awe

If we, as adults, could comprehend
how much we, at times, intimidate our children,
we might be more patient when they're younger.
This would deeply root the attribute of patience
and in the process, correct many misconceptions.

Enough so, to let them see us for who we really are,
sharing the hopes and dreams that we have had,
by revealing the ones still glistening in our mind's eye.

If we could drop the awe striking stiffness,
which has built the fortress around us,
just long enough to see these little ones, standing there,
wanting to know us, trusting us to show them how . . .
we'd soon see them for who they are
through eyes of the child who still resides inside us,
who still speaks the almost forgotten language
of simpler times, without the defense
that puts walls up between us, or the pretense
that keeps us from tearing them down.

We'd also find how much we really love them
by teaching them . . . to love themselves.

Compassion

**The building of bridges
by tearing down walls.**

Eventual friends

Thank you.
Thank you for seeing the silent outcry in my eyes.
One that so often goes unheard that says, "teach me.
Reach me. Make me feel that you value me more than
a possession and that I mean more to you than just a
responsibility. That some things you wanted to do were
sacrificed because it was more important for you to lead
me to the river, not to make me drink,
but make me want to."

Thank you.
For letting me know that it was all right for me to think
out loud, even though it might've meant answering
questions that seemed dumb. You never made me feel dumb.
And that allowed me to think that there is no such
thing as a dumb question. I know now that dumb questions
do exist, but they allowed me to be close to you and, at the
same time enabled you to let me know that you liked me.

And oh how I tested your patience. I asked you things you could not possibly know. But, you didn't lie to me, you told me if you didn't know the answer and that taught me to be honest.

Now, I look back and see how wise you were, recognizing the same attributes in myself on a daily basis. When my own children ask those silly-seeming questions, I recall my own. I grin that silly grin I can't seem to get rid of, and the kids giggle, and I giggle, then I try to answer the question.

So often these days, I realize that *you were* a good parent and that, now, you *are* a good friend.

But a Moment

Where are they?
Where did they go?
They were here but a moment ago.
With searching eyes, afraid of life,
snuggled warmly in the night.

Where are they?
Did they go away,
to search for other games to play?
With minds cleared by lack of fear
of what they'd find away from here?

Did I teach them well?
Only time will tell
of the lessons I learned so hard, so well.

Where are they?
Where did they go?
They were here but a moment ago.

The Seed

A little seed
travels to meet its destiny,
as does man, one in the same.

A concept of miracles,
yet to be,
as sparks of life
unit its flight
with untold numbers gone before.

"An accident," some say.
"By design," say many more.
Who is right or who is wrong
will not matter when this day is gone.
We can change no deed after the fact
by disagreeing with what is meant to be.

So this little seed travels on,
eagerly seeking the unknown.
While the unknown lies in wait
for the little seed to grow.

Chapter 2
Us

Us

If I were you
and you were me,
there'd be no need for "us."

We'd all be the same,
kind of normal and plain,
remembering how it was.

When you were you
and I was me,
before we decided that we
always had to agree.

Friendship

I take no intentions with me,
have no agenda, and expect none.

Though I know
that friends have an obligation
to each other,
stemming from and equal to
what they find beneath the surface.

Where this can go, no one knows,
till the time is right for something more
or nothing more . . . than friendship.

Who Are You?

Who am I?
Do any of us really know?
Or do we simply accept
what all those around us
have told us is so?
Do you question enough?
Do I?

Why shouldn't we put
our questions together
to be applied
toward a greater knowledge
than any one person is allowed?

Or should we just accept who we are
as generally agreed upon
by those who know no more
by themselves than we do?

I think not! How about you?

An Air About You

I breath the air you leave behind.
Inhaling deep, to make it last. But, why?

It must be the intoxication by your soul
that makes me want to know you
each and every silent time I watch as you pass by.

I can feel your touch without your presence,
like a ghost that won't appear.
Makes me play a tune on heartstrings
that I know you'll never hear.

So, I just breath deep to make you last
each time you enter my mind,
and stand, alone, enchanted
by the air you leave behind.

In My Dreams?

Did I see you?
Did you visit me?
Was that you last night
in my dreams?

Did you adorn my space
when my mind was turned?
When my back was facing
the fog of night?
When my eyes were hiding
from the dim moonlight?

You look so familiar,
and yet, so fresh and new.
I just had to ask, did I see you,
in my dreams?

A Trace of Innocence

The children's hour is over.
A time for innocence gone.
What can there possibly be
on this selfish Earth
to prompt me to carry on?

The knowledge of good and evil?
The joining of the two?
From which I have emerged, damaged,
and yet, to myself mostly true?

Realizing that innocence
is a blind embryo,
which is as it should be.
Else I would not have been allowed
the space I needed to grow,
a place to do what I had to do,
and at the same time
keep a trace of innocence in me.
So that I could re-experience it
being taken away, over and over again . . .
by you.

Beasts

He imagines himself strong enough
to handle just about anything.

She knows she can
because *she* doesn't have to deal with
the insecurities of "the man thing."

He chases the beast his whole life long.
She lets the beast catch her on occasion,
satisfying them both for awhile.

Different instincts from which
these two must seek out
what it is that will lay their doubts to rest,
as they each chase the beast that chases them.

Missed Demeanor

If it's there...
keep it, protect it, nourish it,
with all your heart and more.

If it's not, be sure, then walk away.

Don't torture the victim of a mistake,
whether it's yours or someone else's.

While there are no good guys, or bad,
enjoy the memories you have,
while your only crime . . . is curiosity.

Silence Speaks

Silence speaks loudest in anger's claws.
The longer the silence, the greater its cause.

One waits for apology, another waits for change.
Creating situations that will never be the same.

Silence speaks loudest when all has been said,
and there's no resurrection for a silence that's dead.

Nothing mourns conversations unborn
like silence tarnished by time.

For in silence, the unsaid finally dies,
stacked back in the corner of memory,
unable to remember ... why?

Swallowing your pride . . .

causes less heartburn than eating your words.

Toons

It's the *illustrations* of passion,
which, become the lace of chaos
strewn across an unmade bed.
Animated sprawls, that,
for all their pleasure,
are only a part of a complete,
solid as a bedpost, relationship.

All too often, people are drawn into
Saturday night cartoons.
Always out of place.
Always distorted.
A sort of sick joke, continuously played
on and for each other.
Reruns in horizontal hold,
with nothing to hold onto, but for
the bedposts they might have been.

Same ol' song and dance

"I'll promise you
if you'll give me one more chance."

Living the same day in the same way
over and over again.
Changing, year after year.
Getting older.
But, never seeming to grow.
As unused good times remain behind
as a reminder of how it could have been.

While on the music plays,
a tune they cannot hear,
and they step around each other,
and one more promise is made,
and one more chance is given
the benefit of one more doubt.
All to the tune of
the same ol' song and dance,
day in and day out.

When You're Gone

Slamming damn doors!
Instead of opening communication.

Getting the hell out!
Instead of putting the love in
to the give and take
that makes life better.

It doesn't mean a thing,
even when you're right,
if it goes the wrong way
down a one way street.

It's the wrong side of right,
half wrong, all the time
that reveals
the right side of wrong
when you're gone.

Warriors

One parent can have no ally
in the child
caught between two feuding parents.

Only an inexperienced, little warrior,
losing battle after battle.
Feeling worse inside
with each one,
till both sides lose a war
that no one can win.

And a childhood dies,
and thus begins
one more adulthood
always on the verge . . . of war.

Of

Of reminding myself to remember, fondly,
times that were not so bad.
Ones that go ignored, but for times like this.

Of the ache and pain of the heart,
stuck and bulging in the throat,
when the aftermath of anger made us suffer.

Of the fun of making up by dropping our defenses,
each, allowing the other to trespass,
not against us, but by agreement.

Of taking communion of body and soul,
never lightly. Often so intense
we'd drop exhausted, but exalted, beside ourselves.

Of days that worked harder than we did
to preserve the peace. Escaping our detection
as communication slipped by us,
because we flew in few directions together.

Of times when we would both ask why?
With no one listening for the child of anger
growing stronger. Force fed those stagnant tears,
the wrong replies, the ultimatums,
and the inside outcries that made them
fall silent in the night.

Of times when making up,
fell short of goals we had not set.
Introducing a pair of us, neither had ever met,
who had predetermined upon existence, that
enough was enough!
Without ever knowing for sure, what it was
we'd had enough . . . Of.

Beached

Waves rush forth upon the sand.
Footprints begin to fade, and finally, disappear.
Wave after wave, day after day, visit after visit,
I understand, more and more,
that the sand knows no names.
It respects no one.
It rejects no one.
It knows not of those who have walked across it.
It has no knowledge of those who have laughed,
and yes, those who have sat and cried upon it.

Here, on the beach, where a mixture, much like myself
of salt, water, and grit, rolls in and folds out,
over and over again.
With my thoughts coming in and going out,
much the same.

I see no footprints in the sand,
though I feel them in my mind, stepping on me.
But, this beach helps me to remember them less and less,
because of the assurances I've discovered
about those I've forgiven, now gone,
somewhere out there,
in another place,
in another time,
possibly, on another beach, having thoughts,
just like mine.

Bovine

We take a bite ...
and chew and chew and chew and chew
the unswallowable tedium of self.

Then we die.
While few of us realize
that all we had to do was to spit it out
and take a bite of something else.

Chapter 3
I know You

I Know You

I know how you are.
I've seen your type before.
You use it up, every bit,
then come back for more.

You look, and will not see.
Listen, and do not hear.

And if you want to argue the point,
all you gotta' do
is step outta' that mirror!

Toilet

Nothing worse than being used as a convenience, except, being one.

For Laughing

For those who laugh,
laugh with me if you can,
laugh at me if you must.

But, keep in mind
who's laughing with us
when we both laugh together,
and who isn't . . .
when only one of us
is laughing.

Monsters

We've all got our monsters.
Some of us like to watch them on a big screen
in a dark theater, with lots of screaming people around.
Some prefer to hide under the covers and enjoy
the safety of the ever-ready finger on the remote control.
Some like to dress like their worst nightmare and
go out trick or treating on Halloween.
A way of making fun of them, I suppose, and somewhat
of ourselves for being such fraidy-cats.

I guess the thing is, to remember that some monsters
are not evil at all, unless we make them so, by putting
too much emphasis on something that doesn't exist.

But! We *all* need to realize that there are very real
monsters out there who prey on those who cannot
defend themselves.
That there are those among us who dream of having that
magical remote control that would make the monster
go away.

As long as those monsters exist, unchecked,
none of us should feel safe.
Not because we're weak, but because we're not . . .
and we allow them to prey on the defenseless, anyway!

Give and Take

The giver, gave and gave and gave.
The taker, took and took.

The giver felt clean, alive, and good.
Although, at last, there was no more to give.

While the taker, with nothing more to take,
died, never having learned how to live.

Ugly Face

It sometimes leads the angry mob,
for they worship most any god.

It sometimes follows mistakes that are made,
hoping for scraps of glory.

It slips its dark eyes into the light,
no more than necessary,
with a hateful, but nervous wince.

This one we've all met that tries our concepts,
this ugly face of . . . prejudice.

Once Uttered

The lie.
The destroyer.
That which cannot be destroyed, once uttered.
It can be changed.
It can be reformed.
It can be re-engaged, as if to win some mythical battle,
already fought and lost.
It can be pushed around, shoved from noun to verb,
to makes its every word sorry it ever existed.
But . . .
the lie, the destroyer, cannot be destroyed,
once uttered.

A Passing Thought

When I was young, I learned to love, from love.
I learned to hate, from hate.
And fear, I learned from fear itself.

From these three,
I learned what to do, what not to do,
how to react, and how not to.

Now, I know that love usually brings you love.
That hate brings only hate.
And fear? Well, it's just not necessary.
At least, not very.

The Mark of Cain

He could've killed his brother for this reason or that.
We can excuse it all day long, and the day will still come to
an end. We'll still know that it was wrong, and we will
still know why.

People deny it every single day of their lives. Too busy
covering it up with all manner of half-truths and outright
lies. When the simple truth is that we all bear the mark.
We all share in the misconception. Whether we say it out
loud or not, we're all a little insane,
when it comes to jealousy . . . The Mark of Cain.

Zombie

It's as if he drags his baggage behind him
when he goes tramping through the night.
Dreams escaping, one by one, through a
tatter in a frayed and frazzled old tote.
Dreams disappear into the dusk,
a hope or two at a time.

On he tramps, his labored breath
keeps pace with how he sleeps.
Keeps pace with how he lives his life.
Never hoping.
Never grasping.
Never smiling.
Never asking.
Just tramping, tramping, tramping,
down a road to nowhere.
Never looking for the magic that can be somewhere.
Seldom looking up, "no need to."
Never wondering, "no time for such foolishness."
Just too busy... tramping, tramping, tramping,
step by lonely step, through each night, into day,
and back again.

The Memory People

They're in my head. They walk around.
They smile. They frown. They touch me,
but disappear when I reach out to touch them.

Then, they return when I least expect it.
Return, with but one purpose, to haunt me,
not wickedly, or as an evil, but just as what they are,
the memory people.

Some cry out from childhood, with arms outstretched.
Some, from dreams. Some, from nightmares.
Ones that never quite went away.
Stammering for existence as I search for words
I can't seem to find to try to make them stay.

Some of them talk in serious tones of light conversation,
just to pass the time. Time that doesn't exist anymore,
but doesn't exist any less, if only I can keep them alive.

Some of them hold me close, here and now,
some place far away.
Hiding my mind in other times,
which, seem to endure less and less each day.

Some, are here to renew myself each time I renew them.
Those people in my head.
They're overbearing. They're undermining.
So strong, and yet, so feeble.
You know them, I'm sure you do.
You know . . . The Memory People.

Looking Back

Whose eyes are those looking back?
Can that really be me?
Ten thousand times I've looked before
failed to show me who I see.

The days I've lived, scarce forgive
all the mistakes I've made.
The times I'd win, and the time I've lost,
peer through those aging shades.

Lips have left their mark on these,
when they said good-bye . . .
evidence of those fading loves
still glistens in my eyes.

I stand amazed and look again
at the one who looks at me . . .
and wander past ten thousand more,
curious, who I'll see.

Splitting Image

When she hit the mirror,
it burst apart,
not in a spray of glass . . .

but, the splitting image
of herself,
seeping through the cracks.

Eyes divided
in different places
by anger's sharp incisions . . .

showing through
a glass lined face
in the light of indecision.

Where were you when midnight came?

Did you hear it call your name?
Were you hiding in the dark?
Hiding behind a bedroom door?
Were you hiding behind your heart?

Did you see it as friend or foe?
Because it always seemed to come and go
with you having no desire to understand it
and not the gumption to rearrange it?

Just where *were* you when midnight came?
Did you hear it call your name?
As some faceless being that you couldn't see
who could see you just the same?

Did you believe the words you heard
from a voice a lot like yours?
Or did you even bother to ask
where it was you were, when midnight came?

The Edge

I have been to the edge. I have been to the brink.
Where thought is a battle fought between each blink.
A place where life's secretions left my thirst unsatisfied,
and left me mystified as to . . . why?

I have stoned myself with airy-rocked blues
in a place where the Sandman and nightmare survived,
only because I allowed them to.
A place I would escape to and from, only to find
that nothing had changed or had been improved,
simply because I had come undone.

I have seen the haunts and have been half strangled
by hope. So barely caught, the end of a very strange
and thin and fragile rope, which had strung me out
and almost strung me up by the doubts within myself.

But, I was pulled up by something very real inside me.
Sloped toward duty, toward reality, something that told
me what I needed to do, had to do, wanted to do.
I guess, I just didn't want to be made to do it.

But, I did what needed doing, and in that process,
I found that there is *always* another way.
Another what for, another reason why,
that I might not have seen, had I given up or given in
to the devil of inexperience.

One that acquires for us, and requires of us,
the carry on . . . found only in knowledge.
Which, very often takes us to,
but, always gives us . . . The Edge.

Footfalls

Footfalls, stealing through the night.
Thoughts, tip-toeing in the dark.
Is it someone I used to know?
Or someone I only thought I knew
who left impressions
in the shadows of my heart?

I turn to listen
and hear only silence, standing still.
Holding its breath so I won't know it's there.

I try to sleep in spite of the footfalls
that could begin again, and find myself
stepping down, down, down,
one steep, stone stair at a time.
Suddenly, on a path that leads to the deepest
recesses of my mind, I find myself standing
before the vault.
It's where the truth about blame and fault is kept.

Pulling on the cold, rusted handle,
complete with creeks and groans, the door opens
to expose all my apprehensions.
I step in. See a candle and a match. Light it.
And gaze in amazed silence, at an empty vault!
Nothing! Zip! Nada! Squat!
This is what was keeping me awake?
This is what I was so worried about?
All the shadows and all the imaginary footsteps
that I've never seen and never really heard
kept me awake all those times I could've slept?
I hope this gives you something to think about.
I'm going to bed!

Chapter 4
Evolution

Evolution

For love of life
I thought I might
travel its path alone.
Not distracted
by interaction,
undaunted by undertone.

But, all in all,
I saw in part
the imperfection of the whole.
A one-sided view
of things I'd guessed
that I would never know.

Till a dawn arrived that burned my soul
and changed me deep inside.
Somewhere between that, that is,
and that, that was,
motivated and perfected
by the evolution . . . of Love.

Is It You?

I lie in the grass with the wind in my hair
and hear myself ask, "why should you care?"
Soft, white clouds, float through a canvass of blue.
I think to myself, "do you?"

Is it you? Are you the one?
The one my lifetime has hidden from?
Not looked for, but somehow found.
While on my way somewhere, nowhere bound.

What is it about you that I must know?
Where you've been? What you've done? Where you'd go?
Has pain taught you what you've learned,
over a shoulder's glance at most every turn?

Have clouds in your life rained on your parade?
Do you feel you've lived a lifelong charade?
Has a once vibrant heart, grown stiff and cold in you,
because the warmth you've felt, has grown cold too?

These questions are flowing through my mind.
A river of thought in an ocean of time.
What is it I see in your eyes, that dimly shows through,
that requires me to ask, "is it you?"

Is there some hidden influence in my thoughts,
pushing and pulling, turned and tossed?
Why am I so curious? Why must I know?
The answers to questions that continue to flow.

There has to be a reason, and if I don't ask,
I'll go through life wondering about the past.
My bravery and my cowardice will live a life confused,
if I don't suppose the question, "is it you?"

Reflections in my mind of the false and the true,
are mirrored from a lifetime of don'ts and dues.
Looking only as deeply in you as you'll let me see,
even deeper within myself, I still wonder, "is it you?
Or is it . . . just me?"

Love

**Living two lives
twice as well
as one.**

What Love is . . .

is having an uncontrollable desire
to say, "I believe in you,"
and mean it.
Loving someone more
with each passing day,
reconfirming a choice made,
because you had no choice.

It's being able to touch
without fear of recoil.
See pain, and want it for yourself,
because you would do *anything*
to bring relief to someone else.

It's being in love
with the idea of love,
because you've seen what it's capable of.
Shirking what some might see
as your responsibility
to so many men and women
who bash the opposite sex,
because you feel you know someone better
than they may ever know.

Love is watching
from the corner of your eye,
hoping to get caught
so you can explain why.
Getting caught up

in that special someone's essence,
drawing you toward
wherever it will take you,
without really caring where that is.

It's putting to use the knowledge
that life is too damn short not to love,
and often, far too thin
to spend it on cheap hatreds.

It's watching the Sun set,
knowing that, God willing,
when it rises again,
you'll find the love of your life,
still here, wanting to be nowhere else
and with no one else, but you.

It's understanding
that for better or worse,
better will always get better,
and that worse
will always become has been,
all washed up
by what you hoped all along love could be,
but never was, till now.

What love isn't, doesn't matter.
What it is, is all this
and so very much more.
So important not to work too hard
to define, over analyze, debunk,
or try to drain of all its fizz.

Because, those of us who have found it,
just know . . . what love is.

Passion's Fire

Pounding hearts beat together
the rhythm of desire.
Moved as one, to become
a blaze in passion's fire.

Lips warmed by heavy breath
refusing heat's escape.
Gifts so slowly measured
by what they long to take.

Breathing faster to the beat
of movement, one the same.
Inside out and outside in,
muscles tense with strain.

Minds blinded by the night
with vision in the dark.
Speed pleading with each breath,
matched by beating hearts.

Grasping now, pulling close.
Desperation mounting.
Seething air in the night,
surpassing all accounting.

Higher and higher moves desire
through steam that will not rise.
Digging fingers clutch at life
that shoulders hidden eyes.

Sparks of light explode the dark
from eyelids failing task.
As life's climactic song
implores a limpid flask.

Ever slowly, pressure dropping,
beneath a peaking gage.
Breath restored through venting flesh
in passion's subtle rage.

The ebb of tide, washed ashore,
with floodlines on the heart.
Satisfying the mind's delight
in sighs so sweetly tart.

Relaxing thoughts, fall to earth,
on clouds of naked mist.
And the warmth of night hides the day
beneath a lasting kiss.

Secret Valentine

Even as you speak, I'm thinking.
Not really hearing your words,
I nod acceptance to everything you say to me.
Because I'm caught up in studying
with amazing detail, the you that most likely,
even you, yourself, can't see.

The graceful lines that adorn your face,
which have gradually appeared from within.
As if some hidden influence
swelled from your soul,
revealing itself through your skin.

Exposing something about your face,
which forms an involuntary opinion.
And forces my eyes to focus on you,
with your eyes reflected within them.

But, then your words grow less distant,
as my dumb-founded mind returns
to listening pieces of discourse I've missed
with hope in what I might learn.

So that when I speak, that is, if I can,
I'll be able to garble some gracious line
that won't be too thin, awkward, or thick,
with the hope of making you mine.

Conquestion

Was it a conquest?
A surrender?
No one knows.
But, the answer to the question
of who did or did not give in
lies somewhere between . . .
A smile on one face
and on the other . . . a grin!

Extremes

Maybe, it's that you are the extreme
of ingredients I've looked for.
A little rough edge.
A little smooth talk.
Sometimes, mature.
Sometimes, not.
I guess, it's this process of getting to know
what I need to know about someone new
that's somewhat scary,
and at the same time, kind of interesting.

Oh, I don't mean that I think you're some wacko
just waiting for an opportunity.
We're further along than that.
It's just that you've adhered yourself to some part
of my inside, and I like it, and that makes me ask
myself if I know what I'm doing?
More and more, I find you as a thought desired
somewhere, sometime, in the workings of my mind.

I don't know. Maybe, you're all the right things
in all the wrong amounts.
Maybe, we're a puzzle that won't fit together.
Maybe, we're perfect for each other.
Or maybe, you'll sell me out, comes a question
dictated by my fickle bravery. You might even
sell me outright, then come back when I'm weak
with thoughts that you might save me.

On the wishy-washy side of me,
because my mind is all I have to guide my heart,
I must dwell on these unknowns.
And so, it seems, I must explore your extremes,
the only way I can, at least, for now,
by searching through my own.

Dark Eyes

What is it that your dark eyes are saying?
I can almost hear them, but for the deafening noises
of the bustling people around us.

Are you as mysterious as you seem to be?
As mysterious from inside out
as you are from outside in?
In there, where the curse of beauty may have taught you
to trust no one but yourself?

What attachments have pulled at your lifetime?
Often attacking from the back or side
when your thoughts were turned?
Do you want to be gentle? But can't be,
because you *must* be stronger than the bristling
shadows you've had to overcome?

What secrets do you keep just out of sight?
Playing keep away with the shock of being recognized.
Probably because your eyes reveal too much.
Is that why you look away when gazed upon?
Gazing back, only when the look is gone?
Disappointed in yourself for your cowardice,
and yet, feeling safe because of it?

I can't seem to shake what I saw in those deep, dark,
mysterious eyes.
Can't help trying to see you for who I think you are,
wondering if what I think is true.
But, I walk away, without letting on, so that
beyond the secrets you try to hide, you can feel safe.
So that, when I see you again,
you can continue to look away,
and we can *both*, try to comprehend . . . Why?

Wishes

I wish I could sit in the back of your mind
and watch your world as it goes rushing by.
A world looking in with sticky grins,
not knowing or caring how *you* feel.
All, on their way, stumbling from gate to gate.
Not leading. Not following. Just chasing fate,
with fear in their eyes, hoping to see it yours.

I wish I could see my own world through your eyes.
So, I could know how you see me.
Me, and all those foolish others
who try to steal your glance for just a chance
to get inside you.

I wish I could climb into your mind,
simply to avoid your glare. I'd like to sit there
and feel safe from any wrath you might have
that would include me.
Excluding me from all those who are unwilling
to take the time to know you.
Which, by that time, I hope to have accomplished.

Maybe then, you'd discover me in your thoughts.
Touching you, softly, but not so soft
that you'd forget I was there.
Maybe then, genuine healing could begin.
After you see that I care enough
for you to invite me in.

Protection

To truly love someone
is to feel assurance
that your love will always be here.

But, not to the point that it disappears
in the overconfidence
that true love protects us from.

While The World Aged One more Night

While you slept, the world aged one more night.
Unable to sleep, myself, I found great comfort
in watching you. I laid my hand on yours, not to wake you,
but to see you smile in your sleep,
hoping you safe in your dream.

While you slept, I didn't, couldn't, at least for awhile.
Just long enough to think those thoughts I usually don't
have time for, that make me feel the way I do about many
things, including you. Lying here watching you not
watching me, and me, loving you, asleep.

"Am I good for you? Am I good for me?" I asked myself.
Or do I tolerate my weaknesses out of greed? Because,
I love you, which rewards me for being myself.
And I wondered, will I see myself in the mirror someday,
greeting my own expectations with a smile?
Or will I be disappointed when who I could've been
fades away into who I never was?
Joining all those involuntary others who constantly grasp
at straws, and finally, the last straw.
At the end, trying hard to gather them all together,
untangle them, and braid them into a single strand
of hope.

With my elbow nesting in my pillow and my cheek
resting on my palm, I think to myself that we *will*
beat the odds, with each of us having different strengths,
I realize how often we break even,
even in the worst of times.

Looking past you in the dark, the lighted dial on the clock
seems to be laughing at me, I guess because with each two
turns of that very same clock, one more day must fall from
the calendar, never to be again. Each one, meaning more
than the one before it. With so much in life that seems so
out of reach, so out of control, I wonder where I'm going,
and if it's fair to you to take you along, if I don't know!
So many questions, so few answers.

I take a breath and realize just how important one more
day can be, because you are here to share it with me,
whatever it may bring. I suddenly feel ashamed of myself
for doubting me. Because, in doing so, I doubted you.
This cannot be . . . because you love me.

I kissed you softly. You stirred a little. I smiled a little.
Then, I rolled over, looking into the dark, away from
that stupid clock! That's when I felt your hand on my
back. You were still asleep, but you were checking on me
to see if I was all right. I took a deep breath, wrapping a
sigh of relief with a quiver of lips.

With that small, unconscious touch, you gave me
a determination I had not yet known.
Not only to dream of better tomorrows, but to live
at least one better today when I wake up.
And so, finally, I too slept, while we, and the world,
aged, one more night.

Just Like You

Just like you,
I will sacrifice all things necessary
for the benefit of those around us.

And, just like you, I will work long and hard
to preserve the peace,
tranquilizing our state of being
in the best ways I know how.

Just like you, I have a determination
that cannot, and will not, fail
to do what we feel is best for all.

Not only because I love you,
but also because, I just like you, too.

When Onions Bloom

When the onions have bloomed and the roses have died,
I look, first, at the ground and then at the sky,
seeing one as a symbol of tears
and the other as a symbol of life.
All the while, looking back on fond memories of spring,
thinking, "how soon one more winter comes."
Then, wondering where the Summer went.
Hoping to see many more.
Not regretting a single day, knowing that I did some things
better than others, knowing too, that
whatever I did was good, because I did it all with you.

Yes, when Summer simmers down, and Fall falls through,
only to lie beneath the whisper of Winter winds,
I know that, God willing, you'll be here
to share that with me, too.

And so, I don't mind the passage of time,
because you care enough to share this time of year
when the world around us seems to dim.
Which comes to mind, all the more
when I see the blossoms of hollow stems
spread their plume.
Standing along side the roses that have died
when onions bloom, and we are so alive.

Night Storm

Distant sounds of rolling thunder
leave me in awe of its grace.
Filling my eyes with a gaze of wonder
when lightning invades my space.

Clapping, time and time again
in vanity, its own applause.
Flashing before me, a storm of veins,
as it streaks across each pause.

Clouds roll over the falling rain
to blanket the sky from my stare.
As water and emotions drain
into life they'll come to bear.

Silhouettes of mountains in the distance
seem to move between each flash.
Like sleeping giants, disturbed by the sound,
as the storm continues to clash.

Fulfilling my hopes as it fills my gauges,
absorbing my soul as it soaks the ground.
I pay it homage, as on it rages,
beating blades of green from shades of brown.

The Sun is born from the death of night,
giving birth to the light of day.
After each storm, overwhelmed by the sight,
"Thank you!" is all I can say.

'Cause

**Many storms are frightening
only because you're afraid.**

Chapter 5
Through The Bars

Through The Bars

The great restless cat paces back and forth
in the cage of conformity.
Yellow slits peer through black, leering eyes.
Glaring into what must be due,
and yet, recoil at the thought of failure's whip.

The bars of the cage are made of rolled, green paper.
Partial pictures of old, dead men, overlap.
Dead men without smiles or frowns.
Not unfriendly. Not indifferent. No sound.
Just cold, lifeless paper with likenesses of the familiar
to draw us in. Into the cage.

On the cat paces.
North to South, East to West, back and forth, to and fro.
While the faces blankly stare,
first with one eye, then the other,
bar after bar after bar.
And I realize that I'm not looking in, but out . . .
envisioning more than the cat has, as of yet,
allowed me to be.
And so I pace.

Schtik

By the accident of birth,
we enter this world
to fill a space, each one,
with a unique face on it,
with unique thoughts behind it,
continuously trying
to comprehend the gap between
the known and the unknown.

We try to develop a style,
without being too much of a schmuck
about It. At least, most of us.
This must be
what keeps the world from getting dull.

Individuality.
Each of us have properties within ourselves
that no one else can glimpse or feel or touch,
or have, unless we volunteer them.
One person's idiosyncrasy
is someone else's given.
The difference between
silliness and style is relative.
Not going too far for who you are
may be the trick
to creating your very own schtik.

I

I . . . is who I am.
It is such, because I was who I was,
having been exactly where I've been
when I was.

I . . . has arrived, here and now, just now,
with a combination of all things considered,
all my own, alone.

I . . . has learned to count blessings
without admiring them,
and is able to look back
on revenge and regret with an equal
over the shoulder gaze.

I . . . realizes that eye for eye and tooth for tooth,
I must live and let live or grow blind and mute.
And always seek to identify, not only who I . . . is,
but what.

It has taken all my days to become it,
this me that I am,
and the only way that I can regret it
is if I . . . is not satisfied with . . . me.

A Letter to Me

Dear me,

Just thought I'd drop a line or two, just to remind you how you're doing. You're doing fine. As you know, the family is well. You're not getting any younger, but that's to be expected.

We have come a long way, haven't we? Seems like just yesterday, you were looking in the mirror at me and I was looking back at a teenager who had no idea what to expect from life. Funny isn't it, how you still don't? At least now, you're better prepared to handle some of it. Not all of it, by any means, but you have gained from your mistakes instead of losing.

Do you remember that time when you tried to get away with it? You know the time I'm talking about, when you were too young and stupid to realize that someone *was* watching. Then came the day you discovered that it *did* make a difference when no one else was around, because *you* would know. *You* were watching. What a breakthrough!

Well, me, you know what? I gotta' tell ya' something. As proud of you as I am for so many of your accomplishments, your efforts, your growth, I feel the need to put on paper something I want you to read over and over again.

I don't think that it can be overstated that you need to look back *only* to get your bearings, look forward *only* to set your goals, and live life to its fullest, sharing what you've learned from it generously with others. It might mean with the simplicity of a smile in the right place at the right time. It could be with a helping hand. You might even have to lay down your life, but you know what? It doesn't matter, because *you* know the secret, *you* know that there is life after life. That, unless the World comes to an end, life will go on here after you've done your part, and that this needs to be a better place because you were here.

Finally, it should encourage you to know that although none of us survive the race, you have the ability to leave a void behind that shares warmth with others, a shadow (not to overshadow) but give comfort because they knew you, and a whisper in the wind when loved ones need to talk.

And me, remember to look at the stars once in awhile. They are amazing aren't they? Keeping in mind that nothing below them matters as much as being true to yourself in all that you do. The rest will follow.

Sincerely,

You

Twins

I said, "you look just like me!"
You said the same thing
at the same time,
I frowned and so did you.

Seemed clear enough to me
that I'm the real one of us two,
though I really couldn't say why . . .
at least, till I opened
the medicine cabinet door
and we disappeared,
you *and* I.

Note Withstanding

It is with hope
when I make a mental note
that I won't lose my mind.

And yet, if I do
that there will always be a trail
of all my deepest thoughts
to lead me back to.

Peripheral Division

Nobody can't know what I don't know
near as well as I don't know it.

Who else could not know what's missing
quite as well as I don't?

Who can look behind me quite so squarely,
then turn, and look mostly, straight ahead . . .

and not know what not to look for,
because I'm looking elsewhere instead.

Credo

I will accomplish what I must with a superior attitude
that defies superiority.

I will always have goals that will make it necessary
to change gears on each hill.

Climbing every obstacle will become a regimen
that will allow no one human to determine my destiny.

While never losing sight of the fact that I must not
hinder others from seeking their own goals
in the process.

The Navigator

Longitude . . . 98.6 degrees.
Latitude . . . minute by minute.
Visibility . . . sometimes better than at other times.
Attitude . . . here and now, although it comes and goes.
Whether conditions . . . fair, and yet, can be altered
by the whims of change.
Altitude . . . Two feet on the ground, planted squarely
in my gratitude for this day, that gives position
to each decision, be it right or be it wrong.
Destination . . . full ahead. Full of what I know I know,
with what I hope to know, holding back,
so I will seek it out.
Where, up the road, I will deal with pre-existing
conditions, because I know where I am all the time
(pretty much) as sooner meets with later, and me . . .
the Navigator.

The best you can do...

...is not always good enough!

People who do their best are seldom satisfied with it, while those who don't, don't care.

The best you can do can sometimes disappoint you in yourself, and it doesn't seem to matter how sufficient yours actions are to others, if you feel you've failed yourself, the opinions of those around you mean little.

The best you can do must begin inside of you, with an open mind that makes logical assumptions, without assuming too much. Which prohibits failure by acceptance of the fact that your best is not just the result of being the best you can be . . .
but the distance you've traveled to achieve it.

Pity pot

Slapped in the face with a verbalization,
my very best angry friend said,
"wake up! and smell the coffee.
Grow up! without that pity-pot to sit on.
Reach out! I'm here, as always,
just as you've always been for me.
I won't let you fail unless you turn tail and run.
Stand up! and be accountable to yourself,
so you'll be strong in my weak times."

My friend took a breath, then with face softened,
looked me in the eye and continued . . .

"If I should fall and can't get up,
(which can happen to us all)
and you're not there to help, you'll feel bad,
which, as your friend, will make me feel bad too.
Leaving me to wonder . . . who failed who."

All We Are

If all we are,
if all we would become,
if all we would find in failure,
gives us nothing more than knowledge;

What we are,
or would be, or have even failed to be,
makes of us more than we were.

Teacher

You taught me right from wrong,
often when I longed for other directions.
You molded and folded me into what has become me.

And though consolation rests deep in my soul,
it's been very hard, at times, to admit what I know,
because of you.

When I stood in defiance, you knocked me down.
When I kneeled in defeat, you lifted me.
And when I looked for answers I just knew I didn't have,
you found them, not for me, but from within myself.

Now, when day drains even into the darkest of nights,
I scarce can believe the gifts I've received, from you,
my teacher . . . Life!

Seers

We live a life
that would not be
had we not known
what could've been...

because we looked
at what it was
that made us
look again.

The Climb

Once, I sat in the valley and talked of valley things
to other valley people of what tomorrow brings.

I spoke of climbing out to see what I could see,
they talked of valley things, kind of ignoring me.

So, I climbed the valley wall and left the others there.
I'm sure they talked about me as if I didn't care.

But, I walked across the plains in search of other places
and learned of many other things beyond the valley faces.

I climbed a mountainside, till I reached the very top,
surveyed the world around me and knew I'd never stop.

I rested on that mountain peak, feeling so clean and clear,
wishing with all my heart that the valley people were here.

The Question

We humans may have no greater task
than to ask . . . why?

It leads to all discoveries, great and small,
of mind, body, and soul,
and follows us where ever we go
throughout our lives.

Between the first word that leaves our lips
and the last thought to cross our minds,
we are always faced with the great constant,
the question . . . why?

Determinations

When you stand your ground and defy them all,
the doubters, and the less-than-best-of-friends,
doing what you do as it comes to you,
without comparing or despairing,
building the right kind of stuff from just enough
determination . . .

. . . you will climb mountains that others only gaze upon
in wonder of their majesty.
And, because of who you are, you will feel sorrow
and regret for those who will never know or even dream
that they could have looked across at you, equally,
from their own.

Chapter 6
Thousand Islands

Thousand Islands

The cause? Who knows?
Some things just happen beyond our control.
While, other things we can control tend to control us.
The effects of which, only we, each, alone, can know.
And that makes of us who we feel we must be
in a volcanic world which, in turn,
creates many islands with its cruelties.

If we humans are to be truly free to make our own
decisions, we must take the bad with the good and
try to separate it all. Try to understand.
Many times, the mind is all we have to guide the
conscience, because the heart is weak and full of trouble.
Not the pump that keeps us alive, but that bump in the
road when we try to go wrong.
Because these two can't always agree, we tend to make
islands of ourselves, isolated, and dedicated to being alone.
Each of us should resemble an island.
But, only in the sense that we contain, individually,
the many elements deemed necessary by our Creator
to help us cope and survive, if only we can recognize them.

The mind contains them, but is a trickster who can lie to
us, because we want it to! So strongly influenced by a
world gone mad, it's in disarray much of the time.
Then we panic. Need to put things in perspective.
Arrange things according to the word of me.
That's when we hear that little voice. Intuition.

So faint that many don't listen to it. They should.
It almost always knows the answer or knows where to look for the answer, because it has access to all the facts and figures and influences we've come in contact with over a lifetime. Such a quiet little voice, so often ignored.
A tiny messenger that says that persistence *will* succeed, *will* fill the need, and *will* deal with the cause and effect that affects our cause the most.
And that we must trust that place behind the face, behind the flaws, where we really do know the truth, but, also where the conscience must be willed to be our guide.

And so, to separate what the truth is, *according to our surroundings*, from what really *is* true, we must search that darkened room no one else can see. Where no one else can know who we really are and who we can become. But, to do so, we must overcome that delusionary thief who seeks its own . . . the ego.
This conversation piece of ourselves that constantly searches for grandeur. When the grandest thing in this life experience is to become one with self, instead of dividing our loyalties. This cannot be accomplished till
we "fess up" and admit that things change, that we must adapt, that we are not all knowing and all seeing, that change can indeed be a good thing, and that the ego needs to just "shut up and listen."

Such inner strength we have with which to "heal thyself."
What awesome power we hold reserved. The soul.
Indestructible. It can be covered, blocked, diverted, numbed, distorted, twisted, convicted, confused, heckled, perplexed, bewildered, baffled, *and* condemned.
And yet, it survives *everything* we throw at it.
Why? Because it *is* truly indestructible.
Then, why all the trouble?
Because, it is utterly ignorable.

But, because it survives eternally, it is always there
waiting for the arrival *or* the return of our senses.
Simply because it knows how complicated we are.
That we really do know the inside things that tend to
turn us outside in. And that we do tell ourselves lies.
Sometimes, for many years. Almost, intentionally
misunderstanding, merely because we will not admit
what can be, what our potential is, what could have been,
and the fact that we could have been wrong about so many
things along the way.

It's as if we've all signed on to this no-fault self assurance
that we must always be right to be true.

And so, we fail miserably to realize that what may seem to
be the truth of the matter may not be a totally accurate
picture of ourselves because we're looking through a
magnified distortion. We're too close. Too critical.
If we care at all, some of us tend to care too much what we
look like to others. Then, we're too hard on ourselves.
That's when we miss the point. We're all fallible.
All imperfect. Always searching. So many people looking
for the key. So few figuring out that there is no key!
Much less that there is no lock! It's there for the taking!
The realization that no one is *ever* all he or she can be.
And that unless we attain some balance within ourselves
we will *always* judge ourselves too harshly if we have an
ounce of self respect.

What it comes down to is this;
To have feelings for others, we must, first and foremost
have regard and respect for ourselves. To have this,
we must do our best. If we've done that, we're free!
Free to allow our flaws to mingle with the flaws of others.
Compare notes. Say it right out loud!
"I'm a dumb-ass!"

when it comes to this, or that, or the other thing.
"So what else is new!"
It doesn't matter! It's time to move on.

What does matter, is that there are a thousand would be
islands all around each and every one of us.
Some are distant. Some are not. All are inhabited.
All were created with the ability to become one with
another. Available to take part in the great land mass
of humankind.
We must not isolate them *all* from us, because,
if we do, we isolate ourselves, as well.

A Time of Blue

It's a time of blue when there's nothing to do,
but take inventory of old thoughts and "good ol' days"
that are better because they're gone.
The passage of time is so much kinder
gazing through the hazy days of memory.
I find myself much blinder than before as once more
I find them seeping from between me.
Were they liar's eyes or did they change their mind?
Distant times, not buried quite so deep,
get close enough I can't touch them, as if to fill me
with a fog of memories I'm not sure will keep.
As the shadows of times I'm not even sure existed
resist my efforts to remember them.
I don't want to change them. Just understand them.
It's as if I can see them and they can't see me.
And I feel myself pressing hard, maybe too hard,
to know the stuff I'm made of.
I start throwing questions at myself.
"Did I have the strength back then to endure
what I could now? Did my growing pains add to,
or take away from it? Was it all worth it?
Have I grown? Have others benefited from my life?
Can I stand to be in the same room with me?"
Just then, a door opened in the back of my mind.
I heard myself think a whisper from beyond it.

"Yes. Yes. Yes. We live. We learn. We endure.
Without ever knowing for sure, what could've been,
or what will be. But, if we don't look, we'll never see."

After a long pause, I decided that maybe I'm not so bad.
That maybe, there is hope for me. So I put away all the
questions for another time when answers are few.
Knowing me, someday I'll probably drag them out again.
But, for now, they're stored once more in A Time of Blue.

Stone's Extremity

The price we pay for diligence
and the earnest desire to learn and grow
is paid to the jealous and the lazy.
They scoff at, and scorn qualities
that are beyond them, and yet,
before their very eyes.

But, the benefits of sticking with it
far outweigh those mindless persecutions.
For buried deep in the roots of growth
are the answers we seek, which,
become obvious over time, while
growing even *more* obscure to those
who continue to deny their own ability to understand.

Shadowland

I feel a presence, a turbulence,
a gray translucence
that moves around inside me.
A restless shadow of myself.
A faceless, tasteless side of me.
A further essence
that breathes between each breath.
Competing thought for thought
against ones I don't confess.
Which, picks apart my mind
with facts I won't admit
from memories that,
whether I like it or not,
are now a part of it.

I feel the grit of friction
as it slides beneath my skin.
A disconcerting life force
of contradictions from within.
It makes me incomplacent
by making me aware
of all the restless motives,
alive and well in there.
Then, disagrees with me
when I underestimate
the self I thought I knew so well
that I fail to emulate.

At times I feel a faceless grin,
when humor strikes me odd.
As if we're laughing at myself,
my shadow, me, and God.
Then, I think, between ourselves,
"how strange, this combination,
that no one else can see or hear,
that confirms my complications."

I have, at times, been caught between
who I thought I was,
and who I think I am.
But only when my life gets low
and I deny where it is I stand.
Should I voice my discontentment?
Should I speak out against me?
Did I cry out, because of my doubts,
with no one there to hear me?
Did I lose myself in shadows,
no one knows but us?
Or did we really find myself
in the me we've learned to trust?

And so, as God is my shadow,
I swear to be my own witness,
tell the truth, the whole truth,
and nothing but, *if only to myself*,
with little or no proof,
and pursue the things that I must do,
with decisions, black or white,
gray, sometimes even blue.
So that, in my actions,
far from mine alone,
I can meet my own demands.
Because for the World to get to me,
it must first go through my
Shadowland.

Simplicity

The known versus the unknown
with us all caught in the middle.
We long to know so much,
only to find we know so little.

Our eyes are often opened by chance
and forced closed by reality.
When many answers are overlooked,
because we lack simplicity.

Complications

The simple logic from which solutions are born
is often so overshadowed by daily frustration
that the joys of life are easily overlooked
in the complications of the search.

Enigma

It's the time of more. More. More. More.
We have more and want more than at any time
in human history. We also know more
than we ever have or could have imagined.
This makes modern civilization the most dangerous of all.
The ruthless pretense of knowledge makes us haughty
and full of ourselves. Makes us arrogant.
Makes many of us unable to look down in mercy
without looking down, upon.
Maybe this is because in the process of building
a great society in such a short span of time,
we've concluded that, this makes us great
on an individual basis.
Nothing could be further from the truth.
It is the *concept* we have *elected* to live by
(whether we live by it or not) and its greatness
that should humble us to be so fortunate.

No. The greatest thing about any of us, is potential.
Our potential to do, to not do, to undo.
And then to select, correct, and reflect on the
schemes of things. To discover.
To scratch one's head, then tap the temple,
contemplating . . . why?
Then, answer ourselves with . . . why not?

Greatness can be found only in a combined effort,
wedged between what we know and what we're able
to learn. Wherein the enigma resides.
One, which denies itself when recognized,
to be then realized in denial.
Where even those who *have* shucked themselves
of the whoppers and outright lies we tend to perpetuate,
will even so, be amazed, when the scales fall from the eyes
and we finally see that knowledge and potential are
two of God's greatest gifts and two of man's worst curses.

Gods

Most gods are spawned by man
to deny the existence
of the very power who created him.

Yielding to a force greater than himself
deflates the ego.

This sometimes leads him to create a god
of his liking
from what is predominant in his mind,
which, only too often . . . is himself.

The Fax

I am a clearer facsimile
of the me I used to know.
A more vivid copy of myself
a few short years ago.

I must deny the me that I
hoped to find, way back when.
And must admit the worst of it
in years I cannot mend.

But the trip was worth the journey,
though the path was hard and slow.
Separating what I thought I knew
from what, now . . . I know I know.

Criticism

The World's easiest occupation.
Not to be confused with or excluded from
the World's oldest profession.

A Hard Act to Follow

A hard act to follow is no act.
And cannot be stumbled onto,
into, or for that matter, out of.

Because, once you become
a hard act to follow,
people will always want
and need what you have.

The Task

If the answer to every question
came easy,
we'd soon lose our ability to reason.
Each effort would become exceedingly harder,
because we'd lack the reward of satisfaction.
And although we'd have the answer
for each and every quest,
we'd also lose the desire to test our mettle,
and finally, the ability to complete
the smallest task.
Thus, humankind would die
of complacency.

Coagulation

In the mind, there are thousands of switches.
Hundreds and hundreds of liquid clicks.
Check points which gate and ungate a flow of light.
Each person clicks from a unique combination
of individual indifference.
Influenced by variations of personal importance,
there are distinct patterns within each one
to be sifted through.
Vanity. Humility. The melancholy, thereof.
A preservative spirit, riled or tempered
by what grates and soothes.
We search for what we want, but do not have.
What we *think* we want, but don't know for sure.
Have, but, do *not* want.
Or, what we *think* we have, without a clue.
Then again, some of us are *exactly* where we need to be,
without even knowing it. Still, we search.

This leads us all to our emotions.
We get there by trudging through our greed,
where the "I" keeps track of love, hate, jealousy, and fear.
Which, much of the time, are the four pillars upon which
well being, either rests, or grows restless.
Our greed appoints our tenacity to operate this system.
The commander in charge of;
"Why did I do this?" or "Why did I do that?"
Which, in the process,

leads us to intelligence *and* stupidity,
and, if we're lucky, reason or rhyme.
Ultimately, constituting the most profound difference,
not between the sexes, not among the races,
but each and every individual personality.

People. Just people. Existing. Consisting.
Sometimes pushing. Sometimes resisting.
Always on the mind, what we *may* or *may not* know.
A coagulation of influences.
Of pressures and easings. Of grates and pleasings.
When life, as we know it, comes a calling,
comes a dripping.
Sometimes clotting, sometimes flowing,
through the switches.
Some turned on, some turned off,
by what affects us most, or mostly not.

Still, we click.
Most of us try to do it *right*,
(whatever that is)
We flow and then we coagulate.
Using this system to search for who we really are.
Always hoping that, for all our trouble,
we're not too late.

Chapter 7
The Thin Line

The Thin line

On one side of it, I can say anything I want.
Make all the noise I want.
Pretty much pursue most anything
that gives me life, liberty, and makes me happy.

On the other side of that very same line
is your right to privacy,
your right not hear *me*, or anything
you don't want to hear.
Your right to be yourself on your side of the line
and/or behind closed doors.

Neither of us have the right to cross that line
unless both of us approve.
These things are not only self-evident,
but only right, only moral, only good.

Which leaves me where I stand
and you standing where you stand,
both capable and hopefully willing
to look down and see that thin, invisible line,
drawn between us all . . .
where my right to free speech stops,
and your right to privacy . . . begins.

Tolerance vs Toleration

Intolerance is a term thrown from one end of the spectrum to the other. A suspect term because of how it is abused. So much bad behavior is excused in the name of tolerance. If all I want is to be left alone, this does not mean that I don't care, it could very well mean that I'm tired and need to rest, possibly from doing good things for others. Things which have gone unnoticed by those very same people because they were busy protesting while I was helping them out! Sound ridiculous? Think about it!
How many people get so wound and bound by their beliefs that no one can approach them from outside their immediate circle? By virtue of that, how can they have any idea what really is going on, on the other side of the hype? So much of this is about camera angle, ego speak, and "lookin' gooooood" in front of others.
This is where the confusion between the two words does a great deal of harm and a disservice to those who are sincere about doing the right thing.

Everybody knows those people who look for opportunities. Those who take advantage. Those people who just plain don't care. People who would as soon walk in your house, do the unspeakable, walk away with no conscience, and kick your dog on the way out! People are getting away with bad behavior because people are afraid to speak out for fear of being labeled *intolerant,* for crying out loud! Whether it's noise pollution, abusive language that's uninvited, or an unwanted invasion of your privacy, it should never be tolerated!

Yes. When it comes to *purely* racial issues, religious issues, or the battle between the sexes, that do not involve someone peeking up the skirt of justice, simply for a chuckle and a freebie, I am indeed for tolerance.

It's toleration of bad behavior that may very well bring us down if we allow it to continue.

We need to bring manners back if we are to survive as a nation, and ultimately, as a civilization.

Power

No man is so powerful that he cannot be defeated,
often by his own strength.

Having power carries with it a responsibility
exactly equal to it.

Sometimes, the meekest of foes can turn the battle
by turning the tables, facing his enemy
with the viciousness of his own might.

Saving his own inner strength, to be channeled
toward others, instead of at them.

Trying

Regardless of what we've always heard, practice
does not make any of us perfect.

What it does do is give us a more accurate
picture of ourselves, a little more,
each time we fail, less and less,
as time goes on, the more and more we try.

The Standard

The standard by which we travel
determines the substance by which we live.
The attitude with which we view tomorrow
decides the magnitude of its existence.

Endurance . . .

. . . is having the persistence to get where you're going without demanding the assurance of where that is.

Bite your tongue!

To grit the teeth, tongue in cheek,
is to either learn to grin and bear it,
or develop a taste for one's own blood.

It is a learned response that allows us
to laugh off an aggravation.
As humans, we are usually funny *or* serious.
To mix the two, and at the same time,
try to compose ourselves
to keep from wringing someone's neck,
indeed becomes an art form that we are
ill-equipped to handle.

But, as we mature, hopefully, we will find
that magical wisdom that allows the here-to-fore
unknown peacemaker to step in and pick on us.
Make fun of us at our own expense.
Make us feel silly inside so we can laugh
on the outside.

Allows us to mentally tie somebody's shoestrings
together, without really doing it.
You know, those people who really do deserve it,
and so very much more.

Each and every one of us knows people who push
our buttons. Push and push and push.
Over and over again.
People without reason, and certainly, without rhyme.
Those of us who have learned it, know what it is.
Know that, many times, before we even begin, we're done.
That we have to walk away. That if we stay,
we will indeed have to develop a taste we will not like,
when enamel becomes embedded in flesh.
Bite you tongue!

Busybody

Hey! Hey! Look! Look!
There, out the window!
See "those two" talking.
Right out loud.
Right out there in broad daylight!
I wonder why?
What?
Because, they've got nothing to hide?
Oh, of course not, go away.
Hey you! Look! Look!
There, out the window . . .

Oblique...

are the times when I've given
some insight to someone
who did not think he needed it
and then watched as it dawn on him,
only because he thought it was his own idea.

It's as if I won because I lost,
taking first place in the race,
less the glory of the finish line.
Giving gloss to a photo finish, without my own shine.
Winning the prize by being disqualified.

This is when I smile a smile that no one else can
understand, or needs to.

To be clear...

without being transparent,
is good practice
for seeing through others.

Doubt

That wicked child
who spawns
generations of others.

The pursuit of excellence . . .

. . . must be the goal of all successes.
The start and finish, plus, the meter in every step.

It is what gives the journey its nobility,
and its completion an ultimate reward.

For what possible other end could give purpose
to anything less
than the high regard that moves our goals ever further.

The greater burden . . .

must be,
to die, never having tried.

The lesser of evils . . . to have failed.

Convict

But, for lack of evidence,
my thoughts would convict me.

But, for lack of conviction,
I'd give it more thought!

Zeal

If man could admit failure with the same zeal
he uses to claim success,
the two concepts would be brought together
as the benefit by which he could not fail to succeed.

Timidity

Fear, with reason, is one thing.
A learned response, left over
from an experience, come and gone.
One, which can change, for the better,
what some future event might be.

But, timidity,
this shy little culprit, hides inside
and fears what it does not know!
Tries to wallflower around the familiar.
Never fully blooming.
Never wanting to grow.

The Sophists

The Ancient Greeks taught them how to speak.
But, when Socrates taught them how to think,
they weren't sophomores any more.
Which, he paid for with his life.

It's so often the *sophisticated* voices in the crowd,
who try to yodel the serious,
while straddling the truth
without ever touching the ground.

People are *taught* what the truth is.
Taught by a human being, as fallible as the next.
And because of this,
many, never learn what is true. Or want to.

To err is human. To opine, luxurious.
Especially, when there's an audience
that cannot or will not see the errors before them,
because they won't look with the mind's eye.

So many opinions. So little time.
What is it that humankind is to do?
Argue about what the truth is?
Or determine what is true?

Generations

Generation pursues generation
down the corridors of time.
The sounds of pitter-patter
turned to limps that drag behind.

Peeking in doorways as we go.
Reading words on silent walls.
Hearing shadows of those before us
echo whispers down the hall.

It's part of human nature
to venture toward unknowns.
Which seems to be in vain
to then, crawl beneath a headstone.

The race is continuous.
Often cruel. Seldom kind.
And yet, we keep on keeping on,
in search for what we'll find.

But, there's a light at the end,
which, escapes our sight in youth.
Much easier to see, as time goes on,
as more and more, we stoop.

Conceptions

Conceived in the conflict of flesh and blood,
we are all born against our will.
We then follow a path that leads to the death
of life as we know it, and still . . .

From beginning to end, we reach.
Reaching with a grasp that seems so short.
Rigging ships with sails, so very small,
which, dock in empty ports.

We build walls to save us
from dangers we never see,
to have them destroyed by choices
that fail to set us free.

When each wall crumbles
on defenses crushed beneath.
They're replaced by taller ones,
because protection is what we seek.

But, some of us see the light
when our eyes begin to dim.
Finally, knowing where we're going,
having learned where we've been.

Chapter 8
What's in a Name

What's in a Name?

What is a name?
A label made from used letters,
which bonds us to an inescapable conclusion?
Where the first and last holds our identities intact
by trapping each of us between them?
Inflicting upon us a contradiction in terms,
because we should all grow and change,
but still, we must remain the same?

Is it a word on a line that binds us to a bloodline?
Though, we've toiled for a lifetime to become who we are?

Will some of us reach the garden gate, someday,
only to be turned away,
because someone, somewhere, misspelled our names?
I think not, but I really can't say.
Just the same, sometimes, I can't help but wonder,
what's in a name?

Joe & Rose

G. I. Joe went off to war.
Rosie went to work.
When Joe came back, they said,
"you're a hero, Joe,
we saved your old job for you.
Go home, Rose. Go home."

They said, "we don't need you anymore,
we've got Joe, now.
Now, that the war is over.
Go home, Rose. Go home."

"Stay at home, Rose. Take care of Joe.
After all, he's a hero. Take care of him,
have *his* kids, and make a home for *him*.
Stay home, Rose, stay home."

Something deep down inside told Rose that
yes, Joe was indeed a hero.
But, that same little voice said, "so are you!
Do what you need to do, but remember!"

The beauty of a rose is beyond compare,
its petal so soft and warm.
Treat it badly at your own despair,
falling petals give way to thorns.

Some of Joe, built little, look alike houses,
on look alike streets, with mass produced cars,
that all, pretty much, looked the same.

It was partly the times and partly the attitudes
that made people think this way,
but, it didn't seem to matter what Rosie had done,
what Rosie thought, or that, at one time
Rosie had made a name for herself, much less
that she even had a name of her very own.
All that mattered was that Joe was a hero
and had collective-handedly saved the world.

"Go home, Rose, go home.
You, who stayed here in comfort."
The comfort of airplane hangers.
"Keeping the home fires burning."
Lighting the way with welding torches.

The fact is that most probably would have had more time
to worry about each other on both sides of the war if all
weren't trying so hard to win it. When it was over, they
were so relieved that neither took the time to look at what
the other side did and really appreciate what it took.

Which, began a revolution!

Romeo & Juliet

If you're disappointed that your life
hasn't come full circle . . .
If you're discouraged that your time
has not yet come . . .
If you feel that fate has decided that
you were simply meant to be alone . . .
take a minute, invest it in this thought.

Your Romeo or Juliet, may not be ready yet!
May not be finished learning what it takes
to be the perfect man or the best woman for you.
May not have found all the beside the road signs
that signify that it's not too late to make a life,
like no other, with another.

Remember too, the other side of it,
(as there must always be)
that you, also, may not be a Romeo or a Juliet, yet!

The Doll House

The vines climb to the glory of dawn.
Dewdrops glisten on the garden path.
Not yet noon and the doll house yawns.
The dolls awaken. No guilt. No wrath.

The day comes cheerful, comrades in lace.
Chores come easy, long past noon.
Evening approaches, dressing each face.
Business for pleasure, night falls soon.

The players, self-serving benefactors,
lay siege within the doll house walls.
From other lives, they become actors,
protected by the shadows of nightfall.

Discretion, less valor, secrets for hire.
Quenchless fires that burn at the soul.
When dawn threatens to douse the fire,
lips are sealed with alms of gold.

Some sleep early, some sleep late.
Some take time to rinse things out.
But, come sundown, they do what it takes
to be a resident of The Doll House.

The Butterfly

The funny, funny, butterfly,
floating from flower to flower.
Never noticing how late the hour,
or what it takes to touch on solid ground.

Ever collecting nectar
in a drive by flutterby life
that seemingly will never end.

Always ready to flutter to another,
such an agile pair of wings.
Touching turned to feeling
always sends him quickly on his way.

Then . . . summer is gone.
Too late forgotten how very fragile he really is.
With only memories to keep him warm,
winter winds begin to blow,
and he must die, alone.
When, the funny, funny, butterfly,
is not so funny, anymore.

Raisins of Regret

The grapes of wrath have withered into raisins of regret.
Ones that a broken cherry past can scarcely forget.
Those who knew him when he was young
have healed and gone on to live their lives without him.
He stayed behind with only himself to misunderstand.

Loneliness reflects the years rejected
by the paper flames of false passion.
What was felt but never touched, gone, without a trace.
What was never comprehended, scars his face and soul,
leaving a handful of ashes and little more.

Dust to dust and ash to ash, so much realized
much too late.
Soulful reflections through windows that strain to see.
Staring at the back of a wrinkled old hand
with a tear beginning to fall, finally realizing,
after all this time . . .
"Oh, how great it could've been if I'd lived for someone
other than only me."

Life and Death

One man claims that life is hard
as he props his feet and sighs.
Beer in hand, remote control,
changes channels, one by one.

A desperate mother, merely a number,
projected by satellite,
and a child, distorted and swollen.

Sip of beer, button pushed, woman, child, and conscience,
disappear.

He dozes off, bored with life. Just don't know what to do.

A mother cries as her baby dies,
numbed emotions running rampant through her mind.

He can't see her because he won't.
She won't see him because she can't.

He thinks, "It's just T.V."
All she can think about is her baby.

Life goes on in a warped sort of way.
One, with little hope for a better day.
Another, with a drunken sigh.

Which one has but tasted death?
Which one has but tasted life?

Convictions . . .

are only as strong as the inconvenience it takes to change them.

Flames

Sitting here beside you, I try to relax and comfort you.
Shadows dance just out of reach of an open fire.
Loving you so much. Feeling so ashamed that we have no
home, other than this place, under a railroad trestle,
at least, till they make us move on.

With bitterness my closest friend, thinking my deepest
thoughts for me, I know, oh-so-well, that a single twist
of fate can put anyone, anyone, in this same kind of hell.
Knowing that some bring it on themselves, and don't seem
to mind, makes me angry that we fell through cracks that
we didn't even know existed.

Wanting to hold success against no one, wanting to trade
places with someone, so I could give them a hand up and
no one would be here and now and miserable. I'd so love
that, as long as I could take you with me and transform the
holes in our clothes into holes in our memories.
Holes to peek through, just big enough to remember this
place and so many other places and far too many nights
that were much too cold not to die just a little inside.

The fire crackles and pops. Reminds me of home when I
was a kid. Warm. The dark reminds me that I used to be
afraid of the dark. Now, I'm afraid of the light.
Afraid of what it might or might not bring.

A distant train roars into existence, then disappears again.
And here we sit, shivering, damp cardboard for a bed.
With your head on my chest, you've finally gone to sleep,
while the fire and I, share a flame, in the cold, dark night,
and I weep.

Ashes

I don't want nobody tellin' me what to do!
My daddy tried. My momma tried it. Teachers tried.
I'll be damned if I'm gonna' take it from anybody else!
I live the way I want, I go where I want, I got no boss,
I got no bills, and no little wifey callin' me "honey."
You can keep your houses and cars. If I need somethin'
I'll get it, one way or another.

Oh, I've been part of the system, in fact, I've been *in* more
than a couple. The first time, was the last time the old
man decided to knock me around. That was when I made
up my mind that I'd had enough! Hit him back, kinda'
hard. Anyway, I'm here because I want to be.
It's not that way with everybody. I do feel a little sorry
for some of my friends. Yeah, I've got friends, think I
got no social life just because of the way I live?

Over there, that's Wally. We call him Wally, not because
that's his name, but because he's stone, cold deaf, like
a wall, get it? Wally is a Vet. Not a dog doctor. A hero. Got
medals. When he got home, people carrying "peace" signs
were spittin' all over him at the airport. His wife was livin'
with some other guy. He tried to sort it all out, then the

headaches came. Long story, short, the gov-docs said what turned into a long list of problems, including hearing loss, was all in his head. Yeah! No kiddin'. The ER usually just marks *Not Covered by plan* when Wally goes in now. Guess they figure a *bum* like him don't deserve any more.

That guy over there is Chuck. Don't know his real name. Chuck is short for up-chuck. I'll leave that one to your imagination. Ol' Chuck used to be a stand-up, not a comedian, a stand up guy, a suit. He won't talk much about what happened, how he lost the job, the house, the family. Now, his prize possession is a bottle, when he can get it.

Hey Dawg! That's Dawg, 'case you missed it. Actually, it's Doug. They call him Dawg 'cause of one time when he mixed it up with a Heinz-57 tryin' to beat him out of some prime dumpster dive. Dawg's the shyster, the fast-talker, the beggar, thief, and helper. If he can't get it, it can't be got. At least, the types of things we have to settle for around here. Although, if he applied himself, he could probably *be* somebody. But, he won't do that. It's as if he's institutionalized in reverse.

There's a variation on every human theme, out here.
Yes, (to a whisper) I can speak your language if you'd like.
Ya' see, I have to fit in, here. There are low standards that must be met. Alienation in this world can be very cruel.
Our world.

Some of us don't like it, but don't see an easy way out, and it's too much trouble and we're too far behind, to put that much into it. We are actually trained to fail.
Some of us wouldn't recognize the way out if we saw it.
Some, have been here long enough that they'd be afraid of it, no matter what form it would arrive in. Some, just need a hand up that seldom reaches out at the right time and place.

Then there's me. I just plain don't give a damn. You don't have to buy into it or believe it. In fact, you can just turn away and not look at it. But, it does exist, this world that I'm describing, not that far from yours.
And, from where I sit, this is my view of it. Fact is, *I* don't even exist. I'm just the messenger. I'm just a voice in the wind, blowin' around like so many ashes.
Along with all the others.

The Grate society

Grate: 1; to pulverize.
        2; the framework on which a fire is built.

The rich get richer, the poor get poorer,
and the base gets broader and broader.
Built on a platform for those who have,
by those who have not.

The greed of investors spreads fear
from corporation to corporation,
sending good paying jobs to other lands.

Cutting the throats of our own children,
who have even now begun to amass into
The Grate Society of the working poor.

Alzheimer

I search my thoughts and find them blank,
mere places where thoughts have been.
Gone, without a trace, and then . . .
it's as if the floodgates are torn away.

Bits and pieces of memory come pouring through
at such a fast and furious pace.
A face here, a name there,
an incident or two or three.
Shredded layer after layer, peeling back
a foggy tidal wave raging angrily through me.

I try to capture what I can't,
that captivates my imagination,
which, is all I seem to have.
Unable to construct even one complete fact,
I get impatient, as do those around me.
I try to make them understand,
which, only makes them mad at me.

Then, the flood stops.
And all I find are things I can't remember.
I search my thoughts again,
and find them blank.
Mere places where thoughts have been.

Loss

How full the loss.
How harsh the pain.
Living life in sad refrains.

When those who've gone,
per chance could give,
if, by their loss, we've learned to live.

Desperation

To live desperately, always searching,
always needing others
in lieu of
being satisfied with self,
is to look for that which no one has.

An elusive air that will not allow dreams to breathe,
because dreams that seem too good to be true,
will be,
and cannot meet the expectations
that have been blown out of all proportion
into a ballooning need that will float away,
taking with it, peace of mind.

Blood Vain

That which is exciting.
The pursuit of excellence.
What is good and right and true.
It is to search for these that we were given
a brain, a heart, a soul, and blood and bone and mass.

A search that is not lightly given,
because we are expected to separate them from
the dull, the inferior, the bad, the false, and the wrong.

A search, which, by the very nature of life,
takes a very long time.
How long? As long as it takes, providing that we
don't run out of time.

So. If you're reading this,
you still have blood flowing through your brain.
You still have a chance.
A chance to make a difference.
So that generations of your blood will not have been
wasted on you, flowing in vain.

Defense of Reason

Reason
is the act of comparing how green the grass is
on each side of defense,
marked by explanation points,
without the need to exclaim them.

It is used exclusively by smart people
who know that smart and intelligent
are two different words, often confused,
between two different meanings.

They also know that if we *avoid* reason,
win or lose, the prize is always spoiled
by lack of control.

Cabins

It seems like most civilized people live in log cabins,
with the wild and woolly world locked outside.
They hear the howls, not only from the beasts,
but their prey, as well, and simply close the shudders.
Feeling safe, they choose to hide from injustice.

They don't know we're watching.
Come and step back with me. Let's take the wide view.
Look at all the cabins.
See how many civilized people there are?
See how few the beasts are?

But, the beasts know this!
They also know that they must keep the civilized people
from finding out.
Finding out how many civilized people there are.
Finding out how few beasts there are, by comparison.
And how very tired the beasts are,
running from yard to yard, howling as loudly as they can,
hoping that most will stay in their cabins
so they can pick them off, one at a time.
Because the beasts know that if the civilized people *ever*
all come out at the same time, the beasts will not survive.

But, they don't come out.
And the beasts smile their wicked smiles,
and do their wicked deeds,
while the many hide, listening to the cries of the few.
So, the beasts continue to howl,
knowing that the civilized people will never be totally
civilized till they do all come out at the same time.
Confident that they never will. And they never do.

Chapter 9
Losin' It

Losin' it

Being functionally illiterate before noon, I often find myself
sifting through a pile of nouns and verbs and the like,
while most people are tearing down walls in their sleep.
Waiting for an enlightening strike, a torn certainty,
even a vowel movement! Something!
Anything to kick-start the process.

The day's been long. My mind is frazzled.
Here I sit, pen in hand, staring at an 8-1/2 by 11
sheet of every question I've never answered.
Words staring back. Telling me that they have
something to say, without telling me what it is.
It's 2:00 A.M. Suddenly, I have a thought!
Just as suddenly, I lose it, and sink into
the realization that I've lost my place!

I've lost my place. Have you seen it?
It tries to strike me how important it is to keep my place,
but, it can't seem to find me.
I'm not here. After all, my place is now elsewhere!
Trying to think this through, I come to some conclusions.
That I can't stand in line, with no one to put there.
I can no longer put myself in someone else's position.
Can't even begin to fill another's shoes.
Damn it! Can't even drop a hint. I'm nowhere to be found!
But, I suppose there's a good side to it.
I can't blame somebody else if there's no accuser.

I can't take the blame if there's no one to accuse.
If something happens, I know I didn't do it,
that's all there is to it!

Yes, I've lost my place. Have you seen it?
Just can't seem to find it, and it fills me with a certain dread.
It's got me to wondering, if, instead of my place,
I've lost my mind, instead!

(Writers will understand)

The Race for the Throne

'Sun's up. So quiet. So still.
Lo and behold, can it possibly be?
That morning has come too early?
Is that why I don't hear the pitter-patter of little feet?
Do I dare to think that it could be done?

Oh, no, no. Not to get *to* the bathroom first.
Just to feel that I *could* have. Had I been a little quicker.
Had I gone to bed earlier. Had I woke up a little sooner.
Which, gives me hope. Makes me feel alive.
Feel as if I could conquer any foe
who stands head and shoulders above three foot-five.

And so, I lay here, wallowing in the hope
that I might someday be the first to get to
that coveted porcelain throne.
That seat of solitary morning repose.

But, what am I doing? I can't just lay here!
Do you suppose no one's up? Did they oversleep?
Or, is it that my mind feels that I deserve to cry out,
Yes! I'm here! I made it! I got it! It's all mine, this time!
I don't have to feel dwarfed by the pint-sized!
But, I don't dare. One of them might hear me
and scurry quickly between my legs,
locking the door, before I can claim my prize.

Am I fast enough? Am I quiet enough?
To actually win the race between man and child?

It's the most wonderful feeling on what must be a day,
which will live in infamy, in my memory.
As I throw on my robe, open the door,
and tear down the hallway,
feeling so good and at the same time, so very bad,
running as fast as I can . . . Slam! Sorry Dad!

Somersault

So.
Here I am.
Headstuck.
Between the pot and the wall.

Trying to get a grip,
with cold porcelain against my face,
thinking to myself, "what happened?"

Remembering, a few minutes back,
stumbling in, half asleep,
blinded by the sunlight pouring through the window.

Then, tripping, flipping, spinning.
Flailing helplessly, while the ceiling and the floor
did an all-too-quick reverse.
With surprise opening my eyes
and dizziness stuck in my gut.
Realizing that I'd done a not-quite-awake somersault,
and that I'm now wedged upside down
with the paper roller jabbing me in the butt.

Waiting. Waiting. Waiting.
Somebody'll miss me, I just know it.
At least, that what I'm a hopin'.
When, I suppose I'll have just one question.
"Who the devil left the vanity drawer open?!"

Beam Me Up!

Sir,

I am on Earth and am prepairing to return home, having, per instruction, selected and observed one Earthling to learn of its habits. I must admit that you were right, in that it was easier to be discrete, slipping in and out, following only one creature, allowing me to efficiently compile the needed data, without the confusion of following a mass of inhabitants.

Report follows:

This being has a hard metallic body, dull in color, with many scars that I assume were inflicted upon it by fellow Earthlings. Watching it move around on its circular rubber feet was a somewhat pleasant surprise, which, caused me to miss my family, a little. As for the rest, you can be the judge.

Report Continues:

It has eyes in the front and rear of its body. The front ones become highly luminous at night. The rear ones are very similar to the hue that we would call rouge. They flash on and off most of the time. And oh, the sounds this creature makes! It makes my blood run warm. Such a strange language, consisting of a select few phrases, used over and over, inter verbalized by a series of honks and beeps. These are accompanied by a little, fist-like ball at the end of an appendage, with a tiny, single digit, protruding from the middle of it. This exits an opening in its side on a regular basis. I cannot for the life of me tell if its a greeting or a warning. During my observations, I've seen this aspect of the creature returned many times from its fellow inhabitants. The poor thing must have a horrendous metabolism with a constant string of gaseous clouds puffing from its rear end. It also makes what we would consider unforgivably rude pooting noises.

To complete my notes on this facet of the creature for my full report, I was fortunate enough to observe it at a sort of rejuvenation center. As near as I could tell, nourishment is pumped! Yes, pumped into this little glutton's body at a strange sort of cafe! Since its feet are stuck to the ground, it expels a parasite. Which, serves its needs, to be then re-consumed before the Earthling goes on its way.

These parasites are of interest. I've seen many of them, but since the subject of my observations is larger and more resembles ourselves, I must conclude that the parasites are of small consequence. And from what I've seen, they are actually a source of irritation for many of the rubber footed beings. I've seen them try to consume the parasites, but the parasites are quick and jump out of the way most of the time. Although, I have seen some instances of the parasites caring for the Earthlings. Applying what appears to be a type of ointment to the Earthling's body, then massaging it till it is actually quite shiny. But, I've only seen these things peripherally, while observing my subject, which I will now return to for the benefit of my report.

Such a loud, obnoxious and rude little fellow, indeed. In general, my findings are most distressing. Because of the erratic behavior of my subject, I cannot imagine being able to proceed with your plan to contact and share information with the inhabitants of this world. I will include more details in my full report. And just in the case that you do want to try further contact with this being, I have included its name, taken from the tag it wears on its antenna. Pizza.

Reality Revisited

I think I slept through the same hour twice.
Not sure, though. Don't really know.

I dreamed I woke up and looked at the clock.
The big hand was on twelve, the little hand was on six.
I knew that I should get up, but went back to sleep.

Then I dreamed that I woke up,
dreamed that it was six o'clock, again.
Then, I dreamed I went back to sleep.

Then, I really did wake up.
It really was six o'clock.
My problem is . . . is it real?
Or not!

Think About It!

I think I understand.
I thought I understood.
I think I know I can.
I thought I knew I could.

I thought maybe I think too much,
when I think I know, and still,
if I don't think, maybe I won't know.
Then, again, maybe I will.

Pour it on!

I can take it.
Whatever you do, I will make it.

So, keep on pouring. Just cover me up.
Whoa! Wait! That's enough!

Shuns

Men . . . don't do instruc*tions*, mostly.
Don't ask direc*tions*, usually,
till they're lost and hungry.
We make no excep*tions*, often
till it's too late to make a difference.

We do have expecta*tions*, many times,
set too high, too soon, or too unreasonable,
till we are forced to be reasoned with.
All too often, through . . . litiga*tion*.

Only Sometimes

Looking down one's nose
should almost always be done,
while sitting on the toilet.

In this way,
perspective *cannot* be lost.
The obvious, *will not* allow it.
Because of how silly we *all* look,
sometimes.

Well, Yes and No

I didn't say, yes.
I didn't say, no.
I did sit confused and weary.
Not because I didn't know.

I just wasn't sure that yes,
would be what's best.
And what if I'd said, no,
then found out that they'd changed the rules
a day or two ago?

No, I didn't say yes.
And, yes, I didn't say no.
Now, that I've had a chance to think about it again,
I've decided that there are times when I should say yes,
and others, when I should say no.
But, this just isn't one of them.

Just In Case

The dark is looming behind the trees,
hiding from the moonlight.
White-knuckled fingers press the windowsill
down amongst my fears and my apprehensions.
I notice between blinks that the dark seems thickest
down the alley, where my nightmares live.

Night sounds howl in a dozen different voices.
The crickets, the owl, the flutter of wings.
In a broken voice I hear in my head,
I think, "harmless little creatures of the night."
Or are they?
Was it really some hideous thing crawling through
its own slime, wanting to mingle its juices with mine?

Something moved, just outside, just now.
I know I heard it. I just know it, that's all.
Maybe, it turned to a rabbit-like scamper
and disappeared down the alley.

And *maybe*, it was the Easter bunny, after being
captured by some mad scientist who spent the past
several months turning him into a seething, snarling,
maniacal, beast, ten feet deep with claws!

Ah, but that's silly isn't it?
Of course, it is. I'm just being ridiculous.
So, I'll simply close the window, walk over to my bed,
climb under my blanket, and go to sleep.
With it over my face!
Not quite so safe as I would like to be, with one eye open,
just in case.

Jest In Case

I jest, in case,
at some other time,
I might find myself growing sad.

Jest, so
I will always know
that things are not so bad.

Hindsight

If you bend over backward too far,
in order to kiss up to your friends,
you'll find yourself in the position . . .

Where all they have to do is turn around
and it won't be their face you're kissin'.

In The Cool, Gray, Dawn

The cool, gray, dawn,
crawled lazily from the pit of night.
Stood. Stretched. Yawned.
Ready to burst forth with the crisp, clear, light of morn'.

Looked down. Smiled at me.
I looked up. Stretched. Yawned. Felt good.
Smiled, sleepily,
rolled over and went back to sleep.

Odd, Man

White man, black man, yellow man, red.
Mad man, sane man, live man, dead.
Poor man, rich man, one man's got.
Good man, bad man, fair man's lot.
Right man, left man, two man view.
Free man, slave man, one man's due.
Sand man, sea man, dry man, wet.
In man, out man, no man get.
Have man, not man, middle man split.
He man, she man, still man fit.
God man, de-man, friend man, foes.
True man, false man, what man knows.

Jester's Misfortune

The Jester's fortune
lies cold in *his* ear
while he warms the heart of another.

So sadly he walks
as he stalks his own fears,
prompting the laughter of others.

Chapter 10
Nothins

Nothins

Nothin's really somethin'.
Sometimes, when you're all alone.
When you cry out loud
and nothin' comes back but a fading echo.

But, somethin' can be as next to nothin'
as any nothin' could ever be,
if the sound it makes is drowned out,
antagonistically.

So, take a look at your nothin' times
and try to imagine that fine, little line
between war and peace,
lonliness and solitude,
joy and sorrow.

And you might just find that you could even enjoy
some of the nothin' times of tomorrow.

The Wise Man's Fool

The wise man's fool is a prisoner,
but he's there just the same.
With sly grin, cap and bells,
contemplating some silly game.
Sits inside,
beside himself with self control.
Muttering in quiet desperation,
telling *himself* the anecdotes,
with which, he keeps his spirit whole.

Yes, the wise man's fool stays inside,
playing the fool.
While the fool's wise man, stands outside,
never quite all himself, abiding all the rules.

Anger

Felonious waves of thought
slay my dignity,
and crest my banks
to damn my soul
with their very existence.

The tide subsides
when I realize that
anger has revealed itself
for the cruel taskmaster it is.

Making me aware
that it serves no purpose
other than defense and preservation.

I now know what it is,
and isn't.
The purpose it serves,
and doesn't.
And open my eyes, only to find,
it's gone.

The Touch

It comes in many forms.
It may be the serious touch upon which
lifetimes are built.
Or that simple brush of non-chalance
that lets someone know that, "I *am* your friend."
Many times, it's flirtacious and says, "I'm alive! Are you?
Touch me back, but not too much!"
It's often a response returned to someone
who touches first, hoping for much needed support
that may not be available anywhere else
in the entire world quite that exact way.

Yes, a touch can be more than it should be.
Often as not, it's less than hoped for.
But, it is through touching that we must search
to find what we hope we'll never lose our touch
to feel for.

Pandora's Box

Pandora's coffer,
seduces, to offer,
an image,
which must impart
the joy and fear
that drains the tears
from even
the wisest heart.

We're fools in lust
and long to trust
an emotion
we both love and hate.
Because we're trapped
between a lap
which, caresses Heaven's gate.

The fury of Hell
is an empty shell
in the shadow of her fame.
A shallow box
and all it unlocks
in the heat of Pandora's flame.

More or Less

One less shadow on the wall.
One less ghost to chase.
One less wasted name to call.
One less beast to face.

One more time to greet the Sun.
One more line to cross.
One more race I need to run.
One more coin to toss.

One less day left to live.
One more to remember.
One less mile on my path.
One more toward forever.

One day, more or less.
As, through my life I stray.
More is less, and less is more,
because I value today.

Regret

I watch as she reads the letter.
I see her read it for the one thousandth time,
though I've never sent it.
Not knowing how she feels,
because I was afraid to tell her how I felt,
has caused me more internal turmoil
than I could have known any other way,
and I regret it.

My new safe bravery
loathes my old dangerous cowardice.
Macho has given way to sense.
Machismo has moved over to make way for reason.

They (whoever "they" are) say . . .
that distance lends enchantment. It's a lie!
I, in my newfound wiseness, know
that enchantment is *never* lent, but borrowed.
That it becomes collateral, buried, dug up,
and then buried again, deeper each time,
in the rich soil of that garden that is the soul.
Collateral, which is never returned
to its rightful owner.
Because its owner was only imagined.

And so, I watch, with dirt stained hands,
as she reads the letter
for the one thousandth and one time.
Although and because, I never sent it.
Although and because, I still regret it.

The Mighty Might

It's a potential giant, dwarfed,
at its own insistence.
Short on thought and long on worry,
it engulfs itself with smallness.
Laying its one and only accomplishment
on the stupe.
Creating in its master, a slave turned jester.
A serial willer of deeds, undone.

Something bad might happen!
Something good could happen, but might not!
Something in between might not be what it seems,
but, then again, it might be!

Stopping the greatest of progress, dead in its tracks,
with but a single word, whispered out of fright . . .
its own oxy-moronic name, the Mighty . . . Might!

Determinator

There've been times
when it wasn't talent
which got the job done,
but sheer determination.
So sheer, in fact,
I could see failure through it.

That would make me panic,
kick in some hidden force.
And although, I didn't have
quite enough talent to make it easy,
still, I'd do it anyway.
Do it the hard way, knowing that
talents *can* fail,
where determination *always* succeeds.

Little Pewter Dragon

A little pewter dragon.
A knick-knack.
A trivial gift given in some faded memory.
It suddenly seems to mean more than it did.
More pointed. More thrust.
Sitting there on a bookshelf with Poe,
Longfellow, an Indian head nickel,
and a thin layer of dust.

In its silence, it reminds me
that dragons, though noble, are mythical,
and that legends never die.
That people, though capable of nobility,
are often fragile and weak.
Will look for the bleak.
Put faith in the lie.

And that . . .
no matter how many dragons we slay,
there will always be those along the way,
who live with too much doubt,
to ever know what a little pewter dragon
is all about.

Above All Else

It is *in my thoughts* that I find
the questions which lead to answers,
that enable me to find solutions.
Solving the day to day problems,
which, would otherwise plague
an already complicated life.
It is in the *solving*, the tracking down
and bringing to ground a bad thing
that might have happened, but didn't,
that allows me the solace
I need to continue the process.

Situations come and go.
But, if my *assessments* of things that *are*
do not equal their value,
what have I done of value?
Where would be the trust in me?
Why would I bother?

Think time is a necessary part of healthy living.
To be alone with one's thoughts is to embrace
the beneficial, and break the bonds
of a fickle dynamic that we might just trip over,
had we not taken the time to get it together.

This is why I *must* maintain my *thoughts*,
above *all* else.
Above family. Above friends. Everyone!
Because, if I don't, I'm no good for anyone.

Whispers

In the silence of thought,
the pages whisper to me.
Quiet speaks in black and white.
No tones. No phonic impressions.
No raised eyebrow for effect.
Only my own inner voice
interpreting what I, alone, can see.
Just me, trying to decipher what was,
and what was meant.

Yes, the pages, they whisper . . .
of loves long ago,
of likes and dislikes,
of hates and fears,
of happiness and sorrow.

Of battles lost,
of little won,
and strings of events
come undone.
Of thoughts that survive
their own lack of sound.
Only because someone, somewhere,
sometime, whispered out low . . .
"I gotta' write this down."

Index

Above All Else 253
All in Awe 33
All We Are 125
Alzheimer 208
An Air About You 46
Anger 245
Ashes 204

Beached 60
Beam Me Up! 224
Beasts 49
Beneath The Rafters 22
best you can do . . ., The 123
Bite your tongue! 170
Blood Vain 211
Bovine 61
Busybody 173
But a Moment 38
Butterfly, The 196

Cabins 213
'Cause 109
Climb, The 128
Coagulation 156
Compassion 35

257

Complications	147
Conceptions	187
Conquestion	97
Convict	182
Convictions . . .	201
Credo	121
Criticism	153
Dark Eyes	100
Daughters	29
Defense of Reason	212
Desperation	210
Destiny's Captain	30
Determinations	130
Determinator	251
Doll House, The	195
Doubt	178
Edge, The	80
Endurance . . .	169
Enigma	148
Enter Herein	19
Eventual friends	36
Evolution	87
Extremes	98
Fathers	27
Fax, The	151
Flames	202
Footfalls	82
For Laughing	68
Friendship	44
Generations	186
Give and Take	70
God's Apology	25

Gods	150
Grate society, The	207
greater burden . . ., The	180
Hard Act to Follow, A	154
Hindsight	235
I	115
I Know You	65
In My Dreams?	47
In The Cool, Gray, Dawn	236
Index	257
Inside View	24
Introduction	15
Is It You?	88
Jest In Case	234
Jester's Misfortune	238
Joe & Rose	192
Just In Case	232
Just Like You	106
Letter to Me, A	116
Life and Death	198
Little Pewter Dragon	252
Looking Back	77
Losin' it	219
Loss	209
Love	91
Mark of Cain, The	74
Memory People, The	76
Mighty Might, The	250
Missed Demeanor	50
Monsters	69

More or Less 248
Mothers 26

Navigator, The 122
Night Storm 108
No Such Thing 32
Note Withstanding 119
Note, The 31
Nothins 243

Oblique 174
Odd, Man 237
Of 58
Once Uttered 72
Only Sometimes 230

Pandora's Box 247
Passing Thought, A 73
Passion's Fire 94
Peripheral Division 120
Pieces of Me 21
Pity pot 124
Pour it on! 228
Power 164
Protection 103
pursuit of excellence . . ., The 179

Question, The 129

Race for the Throne, The 221
Raisins of Regret 197
Reality Revisited 226
Regret 249
Romeo & Juliet 194

Same ol' song and dance 55

Schtik 114
Secret Valentine 96
Seed, The 39
Seers 127
Shadowland 142
Shuns 229
Silence Speaks 51
Simplicity 145
Somersault 223
Sons 28
Sophists, The 185
Splitting Image 78
Standard, The 167
Stone's Extremity 141
Swallowing your pride 53

Task, The 155
Teacher 126
Thin line, The 161
Think About It! 227
Thousand Islands 135
Through The Bars 113
Time of Blue, A 139
Timidity 184
To be clear 176
Toilet 67
Tolerance vs Toleration 162
Toons 54
Touch, The 246
Trace of Innocence, A 48
Trying 165
Twins 118

Ugly Face 71
Us 43

Warriors	57
Welcome	23
Well, Yes and No	231
What Love is . . .	92
What's in a name?	191
When Onions Bloom	107
When You're Gone	56
Where were you when midnight came?	79
While The World Aged One more Night	104
Whispers	254
Who Are You?	45
Wise Man's Fool, The	244
Wishes	102
Zeal	183
Zombie	75

BVG